WITHDRAWN

ENDANGERED AND THREATENED ANIMALS

THE GRIZZLY BEAR

A MyReportLinks.com Book

Lisa Harkrader

MyReportLinks.com Books

an imprint of

Enslow Publishers, Inc.

Box 398, 40 Industrial Road
Berkeley Heights, NJ 07922
USA

MyReportLinks.com Books, an imprint of Enslow Publishers, Inc. MyReportLinks®
is a registered trademark of Enslow Publishers, Inc.

Library of Congress Cataloging-in-Publication Data

Harkrader, Lisa.
  The grizzly bear / Lisa Harkrader.
    p. cm. — (Endangered and threatened animals)
  Includes bibliographical references (p.   ) and index.
  ISBN 0-7660-5066-1
  1. Grizzly bear—Juvenile literature. I. Title. II. Series.
  QL737.C27H3924 2005
  599.784—dc22
                                          2004021423

Printed in the United States of America

10 9 8 7 6 5 4 3 2 1

To Our Readers:
Through the purchase of this book, you and your library gain access to the Report Links that
specifically back up this book.

The Publisher will provide access to the Report Links that back up this book and will keep these Report
Links up to date on **www.myreportlinks.com** for five years from the book's first publication date.

We have done our best to make sure all Internet addresses in this book were active and appropriate
when we went to press. However, the author and the Publisher have no control over, and assume
no liability for, the material available on those Internet sites or on other Web sites they may link to.

The usage of the MyReportLinks.com Books Web site is subject to the terms and conditions stated
on the Usage Policy Statement on **www.myreportlinks.com**.

A password may be required to access the Report Links that back up this book. The password is
found on the bottom of page 4 of this book.

Any comments or suggestions can be sent by e-mail to comments@myreportlinks.com or to the
address on the back cover.

Photo Credits: © Corel Corporation, pp. 1, 3, 15, 16, 23, 24, 27, 28, 35, 42; © Raincoast
Conservation Society, p. 31; © Hemera, p. 9; John Bavaro, p. 21; Library of Congress,
pp. 11, 32; MyReportLinks.com Books, p. 4; National Wildlife Federation, p. 40; The
United States Fish and Wildlife Service, pp. 20, 45; Vital Ground Foundation, p. 13;
Yellowstone Grizzly Foundation, p. 38.

Cover Photo: © Corel Corporation.

Contents

MyReportLinks.com Books
Great Books, Great Links, Great for Research!

The Internet sites listed on the next five pages can save you hours of research time. These Internet sites—we call them "Report Links"—are constantly changing, but we keep them up to date on our Web site.

Give it a try! Type http://www.myreportlinks.com into your browser, click on the series title, then the book title, and scroll down to the Report Links listed for this book.

The Report Links will bring you to great source documents, photographs, and illustrations. MyReportLinks.com Books save you time, feature Report Links that are kept up to date, and make report writing easier than ever!

Please see "To Our Readers" on the copyright page for important information about this book, the MyReportLinks.com Web site, and the Report Links that back up this book.

Please enter **EGB1248** if asked for a password.

Report Links

 The Internet sites described below can be accessed at
http://www.myreportlinks.com

*EDITOR'S CHOICE

▶ National Wildlife Federation: Grizzly Bear

You will find a wealth of information on grizzly bears when you visit this
National Wildlife Federation site. Photographs, videos, a quiz, magazine
articles, and grizzly facts are just some of the highlights.

Link to this Internet site from http://www.myreportlinks.com

*EDITOR'S CHOICE

▶ Grizzly Bears in Peril

On this Web site from the Natural Resources Defense Council, you will
find out what the major threats are to grizzly bears. Basic facts and a map
of where grizzly bears can be found in the wild are included.

Link to this Internet site from http://www.myreportlinks.com

*EDITOR'S CHOICE

▶ Yellowstone Grizzly Foundation

This organization conducts research on grizzly bears living in Yellowstone
National Park in an effort to preserve the species and one of its habitats.
Facts about grizzlies are included, along with maps of historic ranges and
a bear ID quiz.

Link to this Internet site from http://www.myreportlinks.com

*EDITOR'S CHOICE

▶ Grizzly Bear

Grizzly bears are large brown bears that live in mountain forests and river
valleys in both North America and Eurasia. This site provides information
on their behavior, range, offspring, and the threats to their survival.

Link to this Internet site from http://www.myreportlinks.com

*EDITOR'S CHOICE

▶ Windows Into Wonderland: The Bears of Yellowstone

If you ever wanted to see the grizzly bears of Yellowstone National Park,
this site is for you. The National Park Service provides an electronic field
trip that offers images of the bears that reside in Yellowstone.

Link to this Internet site from http://www.myreportlinks.com

*EDITOR'S CHOICE

▶ The Good, the Bad, and the Grizzly

This PBS Web site discusses the possibility of grizzly bears being delisted
as a threatened species. Viewpoints from both sides of this issue are
presented here.

Link to this Internet site from http://www.myreportlinks.com

Report Links

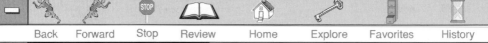

The Internet sites described below can be accessed at
http://www.myreportlinks.com

▶ **Alaska Refuges—Kodiak**

Kodiak brown bears are only found on islands in Alaska's Kodiak Archipelago.
The Kodiak National Wildlife Refuge provides a safe habitat for the bears
and other native wildlife. At this site, learn about the refuge and the animals
it protects.

Link to this Internet site from http://www.myreportlinks.com

▶ **Avoid Bear Attacks**

Most grizzly bear attacks are defensive in nature, occurring only when the
animal is protecting its cubs or feeling threatened in some way. This site has
some suggestions on what to do if you encounter a grizzly.

Link to this Internet site from http://www.myreportlinks.com

▶ **Be Bear Aware**

Learn about the bears of North America and how to remain safe when you
encounter them. This site provides the latest safety techniques and precautions
to take when in bear country.

Link to this Internet site from http://www.myreportlinks.com

▶ **Bear Trade**

Demand for grizzly bear gallbladders, bile, and paws has made the animals
much more valuable dead than alive. Learn more about the trade in bear parts
from this Web site.

Link to this Internet site from http://www.myreportlinks.com

▶ **Bear Trust International**

Bear Trust International is a conservation organization that promotes the
preservation of wildlife habitats through management and the sustainability
of wild bear populations. Its site includes bear facts and news as well as
information about ongoing projects.

Link to this Internet site from http://www.myreportlinks.com

▶ **Bears and People: Learning to Live Together**

Many conflicts between people and grizzly bears are due to careless handling
of garbage and food. Taking steps to store food properly will help keep the
bears away. Learn more from this *National Geographic* article.

Link to this Internet site from http://www.myreportlinks.com

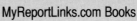
The Internet sites described below can be accessed at
http://www.myreportlinks.com

▶ **Bears on the Lewis and Clark Expedition**
Lewis and Clark were surprised by the power of the grizzly bears they
encountered as they explored the Rocky Mountains and Columbia River
system. This Library of Congress site provides anecdotes and original quotes
from the nineteenth-century explorers.

Link to this Internet site from http://www.myreportlinks.com

▶ **Brown Bear**
Read about the Alaskan grizzly bear on this site, and find out what the
animal eats and how long it hibernates. Information is also provided on
the bear's mating and hunting behaviors.

Link to this Internet site from http://www.myreportlinks.com

▶ **A Century of Bear-Human Conflict in Alaska**
In Alaska, you are more likely to be attacked by a grizzly bear than any
other animal species. A map showing the location and severity of human
injuries by bears in Alaska is presented on this site, along with other
helpful tables and graphs.

Link to this Internet site from http://www.myreportlinks.com

▶ **Denning and Hibernation Behavior of Bears in
Yellowstone National Park**
You will learn how grizzly bears prepare for hibernation and what happens
to them over the winter. The bears' body temperatures, cholesterol levels,
and body fat are discussed on this National Park Service site.

Link to this Internet site from http://www.myreportlinks.com

▶ **Eastern Slopes Grizzly Bear Project**
The Central Rockies Ecosystem of Canada is home to a million people
and hundreds of grizzly bears. Scientific management of the grizzly
population is the basis for the Eastern Slopes Grizzly Bear Project.

Link to this Internet site from http://www.myreportlinks.com

▶ **Few Grizzlies Left on Land Traveled by Lewis and Clark**
This *National Geographic* site provides a look at recovery plans that will
see grizzlies reintroduced into areas they once roamed in large numbers.
Public reaction to these plans is also discussed.

Link to this Internet site from http://www.myreportlinks.com

Report Links

→ The Internet sites described below can be accessed at
http://www.myreportlinks.com

▶ **Food Habits of Grizzly and Black Bears in Yellowstone National Park**

Moths, whitebark pine nuts, cutthroat trout, and elk are the most important food sources for grizzlies living in Yellowstone Park. This site describes what the bears eat during different seasons of the year.

Link to this Internet site from http://www.myreportlinks.com

▶ **Great Bear Foundation**

The Great Bear Foundation (GBF) is actively working on grizzly bear conservation through its various international projects. The GBF site includes information on all eight bear species, along with an overview of its Bear Basics program.

Link to this Internet site from http://www.myreportlinks.com

▶ **Grizzly**

Learn about grizzly bears from this site. Information on the species' habitat, characteristics, range, breeding, and dietary requirements is included. A map showing the historic and current ranges of these bears is also available.

Link to this Internet site from http://www.myreportlinks.com

▶ **Grizzly Bear Information Sheet**

Read about the grizzly bear population in British Columbia, Canada, on this Web site. Information on the DNA fingerprinting technology and radio collars used to monitor the bears is included.

Link to this Internet site from http://www.myreportlinks.com

▶ **Grizzly Bears**

The Great Bear rain forest on the Pacific Coast of North America is home to many of the remaining grizzly bears. This site explains the importance of this habitat to the survival of the grizzly.

Link to this Internet site from http://www.myreportlinks.com

▶ **Growing Up Grizzly**

This Discovery.com site acts as a companion to the Animal Planet feature "Growing Up Grizzly." Take the grizzly bear quiz to test your knowledge, and listen to the audio files that explain grizzly bear behavior.

Link to this Internet site from http://www.myreportlinks.com

Report Links

 The Internet sites described below can be accessed at
http://www.myreportlinks.com

▶ **Interagency Grizzly Bear Committee**
This United States Government group is committed to increasing the
numbers of grizzly bears in the lower forty-eight states. The site provides
a wide range of information on grizzlies and what is being done to help
them recover and flourish.

Link to this Internet site from http://www.myreportlinks.com

▶ **Species Information: Threatened and Endangered
Animals and Plants**
The United States Fish and Wildlife Service (FWS) lists threatened and
endangered animals and plants worldwide. This FWS page offers links to
the database in which those species, including the grizzly bear, are listed.

Link to this Internet site from http://www.myreportlinks.com

▶ **Vital Ground**
The Vital Ground Foundation, based in Utah, works to preserve critical
grizzly bear habitat on private lands. Read more about this group's mission
at its Web site.

Link to this Internet site from http://www.myreportlinks.com

▶ **Walking With Giants: The Grizzlies of Siberia**
Naturalists Charlie Russell and Maureen Enns lived among and raised
three orphaned grizzlies on the remote Kamchatka Peninsula in Siberia.
This PBS site provides information on the eight-year project and its
sad ending.

Link to this Internet site from http://www.myreportlinks.com

▶ **What About Brown Bears?**
The grizzly bear is easily identifiable with its concave-shaped face and
humped shoulders. It is primarily an omnivore, eating both plants and
animals. Learn more about the grizzly from this site.

Link to this Internet site from http://www.myreportlinks.com

▶ **Yellowstone's Wildlife: Grizzly Bear**
This site offers information on Yellowstone's grizzly bear population,
including where you can expect to see the animals while visiting the park.
The precautions that need to be taken are listed for you.

Link to this Internet site from http://www.myreportlinks.com

Scientific Name

Ursus arctos; the Kodiak bear, a subspecies that lives on Kodiak and nearby islands, is *Ursus arctos middendorffi.* "Grizzly" became the popular name for brown bears in the lower forty-eight states and those on the Alaskan mainland for the bears' "grizzled" or grayish coats.

Height

When standing upright, grizzlies can reach 8 feet (2.4 meters) tall.

Weight

Males can weigh up to 900 pounds (408 kilograms); females, 200 to 400 pounds (91 to 181 kilograms). Kodiak bears on Kodiak Island have been reported as large as 1,600 pounds (726 kilograms).

Fur

Ranges from black to brown to cream

Maximum Speed

35 to 40 miles per hour (56 to 64 kilometers per hour) for short distances

Range

Grizzlies once roamed western North America from the northernmost points of Alaska and Canada to northern Mexico. Today their range is limited to Alaska, the western Canadian provinces, and five small areas of Montana, Wyoming, Idaho, and Washington. There are also large populations of brown bears in Asia and smaller populations in Europe.

Habitat

Grizzlies can adapt to many different kinds of habitats, including forests, mountains, plains, and coastlines.

Breeding Season

Grizzlies breed in June or July, and females give birth in January or February while they are hibernating.

Gestation Period

Ninety days

Number in a Litter

One to three cubs. Two cubs is average.

Life Span

15 to 20 years in the wild; 30 years or longer in captivity

Status

Threatened in the lower forty-eight states of the United States; extinct in Mexico

Number of Individuals Remaining in North America

About 52,000—1,200 to 1,400 in the lower forty-eight states, 20,000 in Canada, and 30,000 in Alaska

Main Threat to Survival

Humans, who kill grizzlies and destroy their habitat

The Endangered Grizzly Bear

In 1804, Meriwether Lewis, William Clark, and their men, known as the Corps of Discovery, set out on a two-year journey to explore the newly acquired lands of the Louisiana Purchase. They observed and recorded details about three hundred previously unknown plant and animal

Grizzly bears proved to be a challenge to the members of the Lewis and Clark expedition as they journeyed west in the early nineteenth century. In this drawing, Captain William Clark and one of his men are seen shooting at grizzlies.

species, including one of North America's most impressive creatures: the grizzly bear.

Lewis and Clark had heard tales of the grizzly from the Mandan Indians of what is now North Dakota. They had seen the necklaces of enormous bear claws that the Mandan wore. But they were not prepared for the bear itself. They thought these "white" bears that the Mandan spoke of would be no match for their guns. What they found was an animal larger than life and one that seemed indestructible, possessing towering strength and fierce determination. They found the perfect symbol of the rugged, magnificent wilderness that was the American West.

In the two hundred years since the Lewis and Clark expedition, humans have tamed much of that wilderness. Sadly, humans have driven its symbol, the grizzly, from all but a few remote areas of the United States.

The Vanishing Grizzly

Scientists estimate that at the time of the Lewis and Clark expedition, more than one hundred thousand grizzlies roamed western North America, from northernmost Alaska to central Mexico. Half of those bears lived in the lower forty-eight states of the United States. They ranged from the central plains throughout the Rocky Mountains to the shores of the Pacific Ocean. About ten thousand grizzlies lived in California alone. They were so plentiful that the grizzly bear, which is also called the California golden bear, became California's state animal, a symbol on the California state flag, and the mascot of the University of California at Berkeley.

By the 1920s, though, the California grizzly was gone. A rancher shot the last known golden bear in central California in 1922. The grizzly became extinct in that

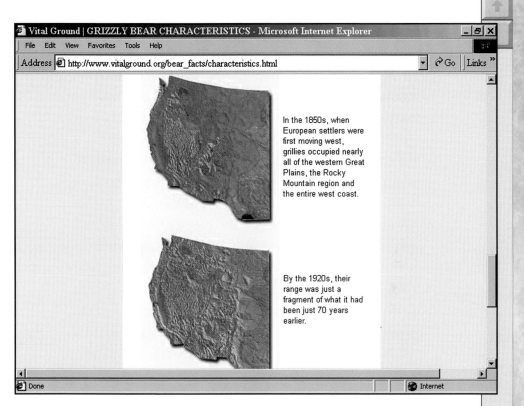

Vital Ground | GRIZZLY BEAR CHARACTERISTICS - Microsoft Internet Explorer

File   Edit   View   Favorites   Tools   Help

Address http://www.vitalground.org/bear_facts/characteristics.html   Go   Links

In the 1850s, when European settlers were first moving west, grillies occupied nearly all of the western Great Plains, the Rocky Mountain region and the entire west coast.

By the 1920s, their range was just a fragment of what it had been just 70 years earlier.

Done   Internet

The top map shows the grizzly range in the American West in the 1850s, when settlers were just starting to enter the area. The bottom map shows how much of the range had disappeared by the 1920s.

state, as it did in most of its former range. Today, grizzly bears remain in Alaska and Canada, but only about twelve hundred to fourteen hundred grizzlies remain in the lower forty-eight states.[1] Experts believe that the Mexican grizzly, last sighted in the 1960s, has vanished forever.

Man Moves In

Predators such as wolves, mountain lions, and male grizzlies will sometimes kill grizzly cubs, but adult grizzlies have no natural predators in the wild. They only have one

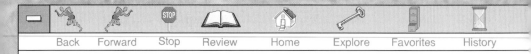
enemy—man. But that one enemy has nearly wiped out the species.

When pioneers began settling the American West, they moved into grizzly territory, and they did not want to share that territory with grizzlies. They killed these "horrible" bears wherever they found them.

Sometimes people killed grizzlies for fur, meat, and bear grease, which they used for everything from cooking to oiling wagon wheels. More often, people killed grizzlies out of fear and ignorance. They saw the bears—as well as other predators, such as wolves, coyotes, and mountain lions—as bloodthirsty beasts that threatened their lives and livestock. They began shooting, trapping, and poisoning as many grizzlies as they could. They wanted to get rid of the grizzly completely. The powerful and more accurate rifles invented in the nineteenth and early twentieth centuries made the elimination of the grizzly bear much easier.

The wholesale killing of grizzly bears continued well into the twentieth century. In the 1950s and 1960s, ranchers in Mexico poisoned Mexican grizzlies out of existence. As recently as 1991, it was still legal to hunt grizzly bears in Montana, and it is still legal to hunt them in Alaska and western Canada.

▷ Loss of Habitat

Grizzlies need large, unbroken areas of wilderness to roam and forage for food. But in the two hundred years since Lewis and Clark explored the West, people have taken over most of that wilderness. Builders have cleared land for homes, cities, and ranches and have built roads, dams, and recreational areas such as ski resorts. Companies have developed mining, gas, and oil operations. And timber

▲ *Grizzlies need large wilderness areas, like this one in British Columbia, Canada, to roam and feed.*

companies have leveled huge swaths of old-growth forest through clear-cut logging.

Western valleys offer bears travel routes as well as a variety of food sources. But these valleys are also perfect grazing lands for ranchers' livestock. And with an ever-increasing human population, the need for energy has led to hydroelectric dams, which have flooded many of the valleys.

When their natural food sources become scarce, grizzlies are more likely to feed on farm animals, such as sheep and cattle. When people take over prime grizzly habitat, it drives bears higher into the mountains, where food is less abundant and fewer bears can survive.

▷ Dwindling Population

In the lower forty-eight states, human settlement has eliminated all but 2 percent of the grizzly bear's former range. Grizzlies now live in only five isolated mountain areas in Wyoming, Montana, Idaho, and Washington.

The largest population, 550 to 600 grizzlies, lives in and around Yellowstone National Park.[2] Yellowstone, the oldest and largest national park in the United States, lies in the northwestern corner of Wyoming, stretching into Idaho and Montana.

About four hundred grizzly bears dwell in the Northern Continental Divide habitat.[3] This area, which includes Glacier National Park, straddles the Rocky Mountains in northwestern Montana and into Canada.

The most threatened grizzly populations inhabit small areas in the Selkirk Mountains in northern Washington and Idaho, the Cabinet Mountains near the Yaak River in

▲ A mother grizzly and her cubs in Yellowstone National Park. The largest population of grizzlies in the United States lives in and around Yellowstone.

northern Montana and Idaho, and a tiny pocket of the Cascade Mountains in northern Washington. Thirty to forty grizzlies live in the Selkirks, and another thirty to forty in the Cabinet-Yaak area. The Cascade Mountain habitat, which includes the North Cascades National Park and three national forests, is home to two to three grizzlies.[4] There are also more bears in the adjacent areas of British Columbia. These populations are so small that biologists doubt they will be able to survive unless humans take serious steps to help them. The United States Fish and Wildlife Service believes grizzlies in these areas should be listed as endangered.

Twenty thousand grizzlies roam western Canada, and another thirty thousand live in Alaska. These bears are not as threatened as grizzlies in the continental United States. They still inhabit about 75 percent of their former range, although they have been killed off in the central Canadian provinces of Saskatchewan and Manitoba. In Canada, grizzlies are listed as vulnerable.

But more and more people are moving into bear habitats in western Canada, especially British Columbia and Alberta. During the twentieth century, the grizzly population in Alberta dropped nearly 90 percent, from an estimated six thousand bears in the early 1900s to about seven hundred today. Scientists fear that the grizzly population in these northern habitats will soon face the same problems that grizzlies in the lower forty-eight states face.

Protected But . . .

In 1975, the grizzly bear was declared a threatened species in the United States. Since then, it has been protected under the Endangered Species Act. But each year, national

park rangers have to kill a few grizzlies who have become "problem" bears, bears that repeatedly wander into campsites looking for food.

Some grizzly bears are killed by hunters who mistake the grizzlies for black bears. American black bears are not an endangered species, and it is still legal to hunt them in certain parts of the United States. The habitats of the two bear species overlap, and from a distance, hunters sometimes find it difficult to tell whether a bear is a grizzly or a black bear. Grizzlies are also being killed by deer and elk hunters, apparently in self-defense, when the bears go after the remains of the animals left in the wild.

Poachers also kill grizzlies. In Asian countries, many people believe bears' body parts, such as the paws or gall bladder, have magical or medicinal powers. They pay thousands of dollars for these body parts. As the population of Asian bears shrinks, poachers have begun illegally hunting North American species—the grizzly bear and American black bear—and selling their body parts in Asian markets.

▷ Other Problems

Other threats to grizzlies have to do with behavior and genetics. Scientists worry that grizzlies in small, isolated populations will become inbred. Inbreeding, or breeding between animals that are very similar genetically, can cause birth defects. It can also make an animal infertile, or unable to breed, and more susceptible to disease.

In addition, grizzly bears do not reproduce quickly. A female does not begin having cubs until she is five or six years old. After that, she gives birth every two or three years and usually has only two cubs in each litter. This means that grizzlies are often killed off faster than they can reproduce.

Chapter 2 ▶

"A Most Tremendious Looking Anamal"

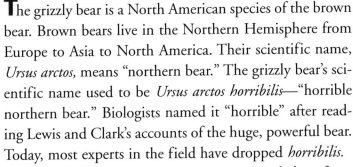

The grizzly bear is a North American species of the brown bear. Brown bears live in the Northern Hemisphere from Europe to Asia to North America. Their scientific name, *Ursus arctos,* means "northern bear." The grizzly bear's scientific name used to be *Ursus arctos horribilis*—"horrible northern bear." Biologists named it "horrible" after reading Lewis and Clark's accounts of the huge, powerful bear. Today, most experts in the field have dropped *horribilis.*

The grizzly gets its common name, *grizzly bear,* from its gray-streaked fur. Its long outer hairs are tipped with silver, which gives the bears a frosted, grizzled look. These grizzled hairs also give grizzlies the nickname "silvertips." The grizzled outer hairs act as insulation and help repel water, keeping the bear dry and warm.

▶ The Kodiak Bear

Brown bears are one of eight bear species in the world. The other species are polar bears, American black bears, spectacled bears, Asian black bears, sloth bears, sun bears, and giant pandas. Three of these species—polar bears, American black bears, and grizzly bears—live in North America. Grizzlies and polar bears are closely related.

The world's largest bears are Kodiak bears. The Kodiak is a subspecies, or variety, of brown bear that lives on Kodiak, Afognak, and Shuyak islands off the southern coast of Alaska. These islands are part of the island chain known as the Kodiak Archipelago. Brown bears wandered onto the

U.S. Fish & Wildlife Service - Alaska

Kodiak National Wildlife Refuge

Text Version

Kodiak National Wildlife Refuge was established to conserve Kodiak brown bears, salmon, sea otters, sea lions, other marine mammals, and migratory birds; to fulfill treaty obligations; to provide for continued subsistence uses; and to ensure necessary water quality and quantity.

- Overview
- Who We Are
- What We Do
- Wildlife/Wild Lands
- Visitors & Educators
- History & Culture

- Search
- Alaska FWS

▲ *There are more than three thousand brown bears roaming the coastline of Alaska's Kodiak National Wildlife Refuge.*

islands during the last ice age, when glaciers linked the islands to the mainland. Ten thousand years ago, the glaciers receded and sea levels rose. These brown bears were cut off from the mainland and evolved into a subspecies.

The Kodiak's scientific name is *Ursus arctos middendorffi,* which means "northern Middendorff bear." It was named after Russian zoologist Alexander Theodor von Middendorff, who, in 1851, discovered that grizzlies were a subspecies of brown bear. Kodiaks are larger and darker in color than grizzlies. But they are so closely related to their grizzly cousins that people often refer to Kodiaks as grizzlies, and some scientists do not even consider them a separate subspecies.

Hunters and others often regard the brown bears that live along the Pacific Coast of Alaska and Canada as another separate subspecies of brown bear. They call them Alaskan brown bears or coastal brown bears. These bears, like Kodiaks, are much larger than grizzlies found farther inland. But biologists classify these coastal bears as other grizzlies, *Ursus arctos*. They believe these bears grow so large because they feed on a rich diet of salmon and berries, which are abundant along the Alaskan coast.

▷ Physical Characteristics

Our first documented observations of grizzlies came from the detailed journals kept by Lewis and Clark during their

Distinguished shoulder hump is really a mass of muscle that gives the bear great arm and paw strength.

Thick fur ranges from black to blonde.

Concave, or dish-shaped face

Long muzzle

Long, curved claws; front claws are nearly twice as long as hind claws.

▲ Grizzlies are distinguished from other bears by their concave faces and shoulder humps.

expedition. Like many people of the time, these men often spelled words the way they sounded. After one of their first encounters with a grizzly, Clark wrote that the bear "was verry large and a turrible looking animal, which we found verry hard to kill."[1] Of that same bear, Lewis wrote, "it was a most tremendious looking anamal."[2]

Grizzly bears are tremendous looking. When standing upright, male grizzlies can reach 8 feet (244 centimeters) in height, over 2 feet (61 centimeters) taller than the average man. They can weigh up to 900 pounds (408 kilograms), depending on their diet. The average male grizzly weighs about 450 pounds (200 kilograms). Females, who are smaller, weigh from 200 to 400 pounds (91 to 181 kilograms). The enormous Kodiak bears can weigh over 1,600 pounds (726 kilograms), as much as a compact car.

A grizzly has five toes on each foot and a long claw on each toe. Grizzly claws are impressive. They can reach 4 inches (10 centimeters) in length and can become deadly weapons. One swipe of a grizzly's mighty paw can kill an elk. But more often, the claws are powerful tools. Grizzlies use their claws to dig for food such as roots, insects, and rodents.

▶ Bear Sense

The grizzly has a keen sense of smell, which it relies on more than any other sense. It has a large membrane in its nose that helps it to smell out food and dangerous enemies. All mammals have this olfactory, or smell, membrane. But a grizzly's membrane can be a hundred times larger than a human's membrane. Grizzlies can smell a dead animal or an approaching human from two miles away. They often stand on their hind legs and sniff the air to get a better idea of what is around them.

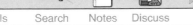
Grizzlies also have an excellent sense of touch. Their lips and the pads on their paws are very sensitive. They can pluck berries and pick up insects with their lips. Their sensitive paws can roll over logs and rocks as they look for food.

Grizzlies can see about as well as humans can, and they can hear slightly better than humans. They can detect sound waves above the frequency that humans can detect, such as ultrasonic dog whistles that are silent to the human ear.

Which Bear?

Grizzlies are brown bears, but their fur is not always brown. It varies in color from black, brown, and chestnut to golden and dark cream. Unlike other bears, grizzlies have a hump of muscle over their shoulders. When the

▲ Grizzlies have a keen sense of smell, and this sense helps them to literally "sniff out" danger.

▲ *The colors of grizzlies' fur can vary widely. This grizzly sports a thick silvery coat.*

grizzly is standing on all four feet, this shoulder hump is the highest point on its back. Grizzlies also have concave faces. From their eyebrows to the end of their noses, their faces curve inward, in a scooped shape. Their shoulder humps and scooped profiles distinguish grizzlies from other bears. It is easiest to see these distinguishing features up close and from the side, when looking at the bear in profile.

But just as grizzlies are not always brown, black bears are not always black. Their fur varies from black to brown to cinnamon. When hunters, hikers, conservationists, and other observers see a bear from a distance, they cannot always tell whether the animal is a grizzly or a black bear.

Grizzly Bear Life

Grizzly bears are curious animals. They explore their environment, turning over rocks and logs to find food sources. They sniff and paw new objects to find out more about them.

But grizzlies are also creatures of habit. They establish a home range where they live their whole lives. Wildlife managers sometimes need to move a grizzly to another area. The grizzly usually tries to return to its home range, even if the range is hundreds of miles away.

▶ Home on the Range

A home range is the territory a grizzly roams looking for food. A male grizzly's range averages 200 to 500 square miles (500 to 1,300 square kilometers). A female's range is smaller, from 50 to 300 square miles (130 to 780 square kilometers).

The size of the range may vary, depending upon the food supply. Where food is plentiful, a grizzly's range is smaller. But its range expands when food is scarce, because a grizzly must travel a greater distance to find enough to eat. Salmon and berries are so abundant on Kodiak Island and surrounding islands that Kodiak bears have ranges of less than 3 square miles (7.8 square kilometers). But in remote areas of the Canadian Rockies, where food is scarce, a male grizzly can have a range of over 1,000 square miles (2,600 square kilometers). The size of a grizzly's range can change from season to season and even from year to year, depending on the supply of food. Grizzlies do not

defend their territories against other grizzlies, and the ranges of several bears often overlap.

Male grizzlies live alone. Females live with their cubs. Sometimes, two or more females with cubs will travel together, and occasionally a female will take care of or even adopt another female's cubs.

Many grizzlies will gather in places where food is plentiful, such as garbage dumps or salmon-rich rivers. The bears use grunts, growls, and body language, such as hitting the ground with their paws, staring down other bears, or bluffing a charge, to establish social rank. At times, two male grizzlies will fight to determine which is dominant.

The Big Sleep

Grizzlies spend each summer and autumn eating, fattening themselves up for winter. They need to consume food that is high in protein and fat, such as salmon, pine nuts, and army cutworm moths. These rich foods help the bears pack on pounds. One grizzly can eat forty thousand moths in a single day and gain 40 pounds (18 kilograms) in a week.[1] Grizzlies end up weighing almost twice as much in the fall as they did in the spring.

In late autumn, grizzlies begin preparing a winter den. On rare occasions, bears will make a den inside a cave. But usually they dig dens on mountain slopes, often under the roots of trees so that the roots can help support the den. The den is small, with an opening just large enough for the bear to enter and exit. Grizzlies often line their dens with grass, leaves, and boughs.

Mountain Retreats

Grizzlies usually build their dens at high elevations, where snow begins to fall early. They often enter the den as snow is falling. The snow seals the den, hiding it and keeping it warm. Insulated by a layer of fat, their thick winter fur, and the snow covering their dens, grizzlies stay inside their dens and hibernate for about six months.

Hibernation helps grizzlies survive winter's frigid weather and limited food supply. Other animals, like chipmunks, go into such deep hibernation that they are immobile. Their heart rates and breathing rates plunge to nearly nothing, and their temperature drops almost to freezing. They cannot wake up quickly to fend off danger, but they must come out of hibernation every few days to eat, raise their body temperature, and relieve themselves.

In contrast, a grizzly bear's temperature drops only about ten degrees, from 99°F (37°C) to about 89°F (32°C). Its heart rate falls from forty or fifty beats per minute to

▲ Their hibernation is not so deep that grizzlies always sleep throughout a winter. The loud noise of a snowmobile may have startled this bear into leaving his den.

about ten, and its breathing from six to ten breaths a minute to less than two. Grizzlies are not hibernating so deeply that they cannot stir. When danger is near, they can wake up and defend themselves. They can also be awakened by the noise of human activities, such as the loud buzzing of snowmobiles. Some grizzlies do not store enough fat to see them through the entire winter. These bears, usually young inexperienced grizzlies, will rouse themselves and go in search of food. But most grizzlies do not eat all winter. They also do not wake up to urinate or defecate. Their bodies recycle urine into protein and break down carbohydrates and fats into water so the bears do not become dehydrated.

In the spring, grizzlies emerge from their dens. Their metabolism is sluggish, and at first they have no appetite. But they must soon begin eating, because grizzlies lose about 40 percent of their body weight during hibernation. Most of that weight loss is fat. The bears lose very little muscle. But they must eat to replace that weight. Their first food in the spring usually consists

◀ *Grizzly cubs usually stay under the protective care of their mothers for three years or so.*

of the carcasses of animals such as deer and elk that did not survive the winter.

▶ Grizzly Cubs

Grizzlies mate in early summer, but the cubs do not begin to develop right away. When a female grizzly breeds, the newly fertilized eggs in her uterus do not immediately implant themselves in the uterine lining. The fertilized eggs stay undeveloped in a process known as delayed implantation as the bear fattens itself up and builds a den. If the female grizzly is healthy and has stored enough fat in her body to see her through the winter, the eggs will implant themselves during hibernation. They will then begin developing into cubs. If the female bear is not healthy or fat enough, the eggs will not develop. They will be absorbed back into her body.

Female grizzlies give birth in late winter, while they are still hibernating. The average litter is two cubs, although a female can have as few as one or as many as four. The newborn cubs weigh only about one pound (less than one kilogram) apiece. They are nearly hairless, help-less, toothless, and blind. They nurse from their mother and begin growing while she is still hibernating

The mother and her cubs emerge from their den in the spring, when the cubs are about three months old. At this stage, the cubs weigh from 5 to 7 pounds (2 to 3 kilograms). Their eyes have opened, and they have grown a fur coat.

Cubs usually stay with their mother for up to three years, although cubs in the Canadian Rockies will stay up to five years. The mother teaches her cubs where to find food and how to survive. When the young grizzlies are

two to three years old, they go off on their own as adults so that the mother grizzly can give birth to another litter.

The Grizzly's Ecosystem

Grizzly bears are adaptable. They can live in many different habitats and eat many different kinds of food. When one food source is not available, they quickly find another food source.

But changes in their environment can also have a big impact on grizzlies. When people spray pesticide on the Great Plains to kill the larvae of army cutworm moths, it affects grizzlies in Yellowstone National Park. When these larvae become moths, they take wing, fly west into the Rocky Mountains, and become an important food source for the Yellowstone grizzlies.

Another of the Yellowstone grizzlies' favorite foods is the cutthroat trout found in Yellowstone Lake. But within the last decade, nonnative lake trout were illegally dumped into the lake. These larger lake trout may make a better catch for people fishing, but they are not better for grizzlies. Lake trout eat cutthroat trout, leaving fewer cutthroats for the grizzlies. And lake trout cannot replace cutthroat trout in the grizzlies' diet because lake trout swim in deeper waters, where the bears cannot catch them.

Grizzlies also feast on the nuts from whitebark pinecones. But a fungus that causes a disease called white pine blister rust is spreading through the forests of the western United States, killing whitebark pines. The United States Forest Service has begun planting new strains of whitebark pines that can resist the fungus.

Just as the environment has an impact on grizzlies, grizzlies have an impact on their environment. When they dig for roots and rodents, grizzlies turn up the soil the way

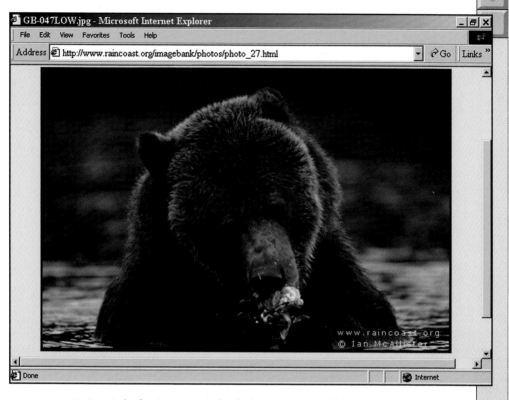

▲ *A grizzly feasts on a seafood dinner. One wildlife researcher who watched a female grizzly catch cutthroat trout in Yellowstone counted one hundred fish eaten by the bear during the day.*

a gardener may till his garden. This releases nitrogen in the lower levels of the soil. Plants grow better in this nitrogen-rich dirt. Grizzlies also eat a lot of berries and other plants, which means they excrete a lot of seeds. Since they spread these seeds as they roam, new plants can take root in different areas. When grizzlies feast on salmon, they leave the remains of the salmon on the forest floor, alongside the streams. Plants grow better here, too, where the soil has been fertilized by the fish.

Chapter 4 ▶

The Mythical Grizzly

Native Americans had an abiding respect for the large brown bears that roamed the lands they also inhabited. Many tribes believed grizzlies were closely related to humans. Some tribes believed their people descended from grizzlies. Other tribes believed they were the offspring of an ancient woman or man who married a grizzly bear. The Menominee sometimes referred to the grizzly as "Elder Brother," while the Sauk called the bear "Old Man."[1] The Yosemite Indians even named themselves after the bears: In their language, *Yosemite* means "grizzly bear."[2] Many tribes would not kill or eat grizzlies because they thought of them as human, or part human. To their way of thinking, skinning a grizzly would have amounted to an act of cannibalism. Bears looked too much like humans, especially when they were skinned.[3]

◀ Many American Indians revered the grizzly, and some, like Piegan chief Grizzly Bear, even took the animal's name.

The "Gentleman"

Meriwether Lewis saw similarities between man and bear, too, but that likeness did not keep him or the rest of the Corps of Discovery from a healthy fear of the brown bears they encountered on their expedition. In his journal, Lewis referred to one grizzly as a "monstrous beast."[4] He then went on to make a humorous reference to the bear, writing, "I must confess that I do not like the gentleman and had reather fight two Indians than one bear."[5] Throughout the expedition, black and brown bears were routinely killed for their skins, meat, and oil as well as for the thrill of the hunt.

Human Traits

Grizzlies do share some traits with humans. Like humans, grizzly bears are omnivores, which means they eat animals and plants. Grizzlies have very long canine, or eye, teeth. These teeth, which grow up to 2 inches (5 centimeters) in length, are good for tearing meat. Their molars, the teeth toward the back of the mouth, are wide and flat, good for chewing and grinding grass, berries, and other plant food. Scientists can determine how old a grizzly is by studying a cross section of its tooth root. Grizzly teeth are like trees—they grow a new ring each year.

Like humans, grizzlies can stand upright on their hind legs. They can also sit upright on their bottoms. Grizzlies and humans both walk on flat feet, with their heels and toes touching the ground.

Grizzlies are also smart creatures with large brains. They learn things quickly and remember them for a long time. A grizzly mother teaches her cubs where to find food when they are young. The bears remember where

Grizzlies are intelligent creatures who have been known to hide their tracks to keep from being followed.

these food sources are, even though they may travel several hundred miles or more throughout their lives. Grizzlies are also known to use tricks to keep from being followed. They hide in places where they can see but not be seen. They walk backward over old tracks and wade into streams to keep from leaving new tracks.

Bear Fact and Fiction

Many myths and legends have grown up around grizzlies. One common misconception is that grizzlies have poor eyesight. This idea may have come about because their eyes are so small compared to their enormous heads. While grizzlies do rely on their sense of smell more than on their sense of sight, they see about as well as humans do. They do not have good distance vision, but their forward-facing eyes give them good depth perception. Scientists also believe grizzlies can distinguish colors.

Many myths have sprung up about how to escape an attacking grizzly bear. One myth is that grizzlies cannot run downhill. Because they are so big and bulky, grizzlies appear slow, but they are agile and quick, uphill or downhill. They can run 35 to 40 miles per hour (56 to 64 kilometers per hour) for short distances, which is much faster than humans can run.

Another myth is that grizzlies cannot climb trees. Grizzlies are heavy, and their long claws are more flat than curved, so they do not climb trees as well as other bear species, such as black bears. But grizzlies can climb, so scurrying up a tree is not a good way to escape a grizzly bear.

Many people believe grizzlies are vicious, bloodthirsty killers. This belief caused people to slaughter grizzly bears during the 1800s and early 1900s. The truth is, however, that grizzly attacks are rare. Grizzlies try to avoid people. They usually run away when they hear or smell humans approaching. If a grizzly attacks, it is usually because the bear feels threatened or thinks its cubs or its food is threatened.

Some people think that if a grizzly snorts, growls, and paws the ground, or if it stands upright, it is getting ready to charge. But bears stand up just to see or smell better. When a grizzly uses threatening sounds and body language, it is to scare a person away. When a grizzly charges, it runs

Female grizzlies are not usually aggressive—that is, unless their cubs are threatened.

on all four legs with its head down. Such charges are often a bluff. The grizzly will run straight toward the human, as if it were going to attack, then veer off at the last moment. It is the bear's way of warning the human to leave.

One observation about grizzlies is accurate. If a human mother is very protective of her children, she may be likened to a mother bear defending her cubs. Female grizzlies become very aggressive if they think their cubs are in danger. In fact, a female grizzly with cubs is more likely to attack than any other grizzly bear. A female will fight a male grizzly twice her size to defend her cubs.

▶ Hungry As a Bear

If someone is very hungry, he may say, "I am as hungry as a bear." This is another saying that has a basis in the truth: Grizzlies are huge bears with huge appetites. They can eat from 26 to 35 pounds (12 to 16 kilograms) of food each day. They forage constantly, sometimes spending sixteen to twenty hours a day searching for food.

Grizzlies are predators. They certainly kill prey such as deer, elk, and squirrels. They also eat carrion, prey that is already dead. Sometimes they take killed prey away from other predators, such as wolves or mountain lions. Grizzlies are also good fishers, and large groups of grizzlies often come together on rivers where a lot of salmon are running. But grizzlies forage more than they hunt. Plants and insects make up 90 percent of their diet. Grizzlies eat pine nuts, grass, leaves, flowers, roots, and berries, as well as ants, moths, grubs, and other insects. And, just as in stories, grizzlies eat honey. In fact, grizzly bears will eat nearly anything—and eat a lot of it.

Saving the Grizzly

By the 1950s, biologists and other concerned people realized that without help, grizzlies would vanish from the lower forty-eight states. They also realized that they knew very little about the big bears. Before they could help grizzlies survive, they needed to learn as much as they could about them.

▶ The Craighead Study

In 1959, wildlife scientists and twin brothers Frank and John Craighead began the first major study of grizzly bears. The Craigheads led a team of researchers who tracked, trapped, and tagged grizzlies in Yellowstone National Park for over a decade.

In 1961, the Craigheads made history by using the first radio collar on a grizzly. They captured a female nicknamed Marian and attached the radio collar around her neck. The collar transmitted a radio signal the researchers were able to pick up on a portable receiver from several miles away.

During the 1960s, the Craigheads radio-collared nearly fifty Yellowstone grizzlies. Each collar sent out a unique radio signal, allowing the researchers to track individual bears. The Craigheads learned about grizzly home ranges, behavior, and reproduction.

They also learned that the garbage dumps in Yellowstone were turning grizzlies into problem bears. Park officials knew the dumps were a prime feeding

Current status of remaining grizzlies in the lower forty- eight states.

In 1975, the grizzly was listed as "threatened" under the Endangered Species Act and afforded federal protection. Since that time the grizzly has maintained a tenuous foothold in the Yellowstone region. While public support for grizzly protection is strong, the long-term well being of the Yellowstone grizzly population remains uncertain.

Distribution of the remaining populations

The Yellowstone Ecosystem is the home of the grizzly, whose year-round range may encompass up to 1,500 square miles. Encompassing more than 10 million acres, the Yellowstone Ecosystem includes the mountains, valleys, lakes and forests that are in and around Yellowstone National Park. While the Yellowstone Ecosystem is one of the largest relatively intact wildland areas remaining in the temperate zone of the world, it is geographically isolated from other wildland areas in the lower 48 states. Thus, Yellowstone's grizzly bears are isolated from the other remaining grizzly populations in the U.S.

▲ The grizzlies that make Yellowstone and the surrounding areas their home have a year-round range of up to 1,500 miles.

ground for grizzlies. They even built bleachers beside the dumps so that park visitors could watch the bears who gathered there to feed. But garbage dumps were teaching grizzlies to associate people with food. The Craigheads recommended closing the dumps gradually over a period of ten years so that the grizzlies could get used to finding food in other places. They were afraid that closing the dumps all at once would create problem bears.

But park officials decided to close the dumps more quickly. The Craigheads protested, which brought them into conflict with Yellowstone officials. In 1971, the Craigheads' groundbreaking grizzly study came to an end.

Sadly, the Craigheads were right. When Yellowstone National Park abruptly closed its dumps, grizzlies began wandering into campsites, looking for food. Over the next few years, park rangers killed over a hundred of these problem bears, including Marian, the Craigheads' first radio-collared grizzly.

▷ Ongoing Steps

In the years since the Craigheads began their research in Yellowstone, other scientists, government agencies, and conservation organizations have studied and tried to save the grizzly. In 1975, the United States government declared the grizzly a threatened species under the Endangered Species Act. Grizzlies are also protected by the Convention on International Trade in Endangered Species of Wild Fauna and Flora (CITES), a treaty that bans the international trade of endangered plants and animals. CITES places grizzlies in Appendix II, its list of species that could become endangered without international trade regulations.

In 1982, the United States Fish and Wildlife Service developed a Grizzly Bear Recovery Plan. The plan's goal is to raise the grizzly population in the lower forty-eight states to at least 1,500 bears and make sure these grizzlies can survive on their own. In 1983, the National Park Service, the United States Fish and Wildlife Service, and the United States Forest Service formed the Interagency Grizzly Bear Committee (IGBC). The states of Idaho, Montana, Washington, and Wyoming and the Canadian provinces of British Columbia and Alberta joined the IGBC soon afterward. The IGBC coordinates grizzly research and promotes grizzly protection strategies, such as closing garbage dumps and logging roads.

Back   Forward   Stop   Review   Home   Explore   Favorites   History

▲ Conservation organizations including the National Wildlife Federation are working to preserve the habitat of the grizzly bear.

Roadways and highways are a problem for grizzlies in several ways. Since the bears usually will not venture within a quarter mile (0.4 kilometer) of a road, the roads carve the grizzly's habitat into much smaller chunks, making it more difficult for the bear to find food. When bears do try to cross roads, highways, or railroad tracks, they can be killed by passing cars, trucks, and trains. In addition, logging and mining roads make it easier for poachers to venture deep into remote grizzly habitats.

Yellowstone and Glacier national parks have begun closing some logging and mining roads. They have plowed the roads under and replanted them with vegetation so that grizzlies will not avoid them and poachers cannot use them. In Canada, the Trans-Canada Highway runs through prime grizzly habitat. The Canadian government built wide, grassy overpasses across the highway so that grizzlies and other species could cross unharmed. Male grizzlies use these overpasses, but females will not, much to the puzzlement of wildlife experts.

▶ Educating People . . . and Bears?

National parks and private conservation organizations both realize that education is the key to saving grizzlies. Both try to teach people how to live safely in grizzly country. Parks ban visitors from feeding the bears. As experts warn, "a fed bear is a dead bear." Grizzlies that associate people with food become problem bears, and problem bears do not survive. The parks warn campers and hikers to keep food and garbage in bear-proof containers. Hunters and fishers are warned to quickly remove their catch and not leave any parts of the fish or killed game behind. People who live near grizzly habitats must keep food and garbage, as well as pet food, livestock feed, and birdseed, locked safely away from bears. Experts advise hikers to hike in groups of three or more, to be on the lookout for fresh signs of bears, and to make noise so they do not surprise bears.

Since grizzly bears are intelligent, highly trainable animals, some researchers have tried to teach grizzlies to stay away from people. They have set up fake campsites and then blasted bears that wandered into the sites with pepper spray, rubber bullets, beanbags, electric shocks, or loud noises. They have also used Karelian bear dogs to chase grizzlies from campsites.

These techniques, known as aversive conditioning, may save the lives of grizzlies that could otherwise become

problem bears. But aversive conditioning is expensive and controversial. Many wildlife experts believe that humans should adapt to bears rather than trying to get bears to adapt to humans. Others worry that aversive conditioning puts too much stress on grizzlies, which makes them feel threatened and more likely to attack humans.

▷ The Bitterroots

Grizzlies once roamed the Bitterroot Mountains in central Idaho and western Montana. Although grizzly tracks have not been found there since 1946, recent studies show the Bitterroot ecosystem is the perfect habitat for grizzlies.

▲ *Habitat for grizzlies continues to shrink as the development of large areas of wilderness increases.*

In the 1990s, the United States Fish and Wildlife Service came up with a plan to reintroduce grizzlies into the Bitterroots. Beginning in 2002, they planned to release four to six grizzlies into the mountains each year for five years. These bears would come from British Columbia, Yellowstone, and the Northern Continental Divide. All released bears would wear radio collars so that their movements could be tracked. Experts were hopeful that within fifty to one hundred years, the grizzly population in the Bitterroots would reach three hundred bears.

The Bitterroot plan would boost the total number of grizzlies in the lower forty-eight states by over 25 percent. It would also help the five other grizzly populations survive. Yellowstone lies hundreds of miles south and east of other grizzly habitats. Biologists fear that Yellowstone bears could become inbred. The Bitterroots, located between Yellowstone and other habitats, would provide an important link between isolated grizzly populations.

According to the reintroduction plan, a Citizens' Management Committee would manage the Bitterroot grizzly population. The committee would consider the needs of the bears along with the needs of the people and industries that also reside in the mountains. The Bitterroot plan gained support from conservation groups and the Nez Percé Indian tribe. It was even supported by logging, mining, ranching, oil, and gas industries. A majority of the people living in the Bitterroot area also supported the plan.

But congressmen from Montana and Idaho opposed it, and in 2001, the governor of Idaho sued to stop the reintroduction of what he referred to as "massive, flesh-eating carnivores" in the Bitterroot Mountains.[6] As a result of these actions, the United States Fish and Wildlife Service abandoned the Bitterroot plan.

▶ The Future

In the last fifty years, most grizzly recovery efforts have centered on Yellowstone National Park, and those efforts are paying off. In 1983, about thirty female grizzlies lived in Yellowstone. By 2003, that number had increased to over one hundred. In recent years, researchers have spotted grizzlies in areas of the Yellowstone ecosystem where they had not been seen in decades. Yellowstone has the most stable grizzly population in the lower forty-eight states. Private conservation organizations including the North American Bear Center, the Eastern Slopes Grizzly Bear Project, and the National Wildlife Federation are also involved in trying to save the grizzly.

Many wildlife biologists believe grizzly bears have a good chance of recovering. The most difficult challenge they face in saving the grizzly is changing people's attitudes about the bears. In some ways, attitudes toward grizzlies have not changed much since the 1800s. Grizzly attacks are rare, and grizzlies seldom kill livestock, but many people are still afraid of these bears. Others do not want the protection of grizzlies to interfere with their logging and mining operations or their plans to develop grizzly habitat. If wildlife experts can overcome these hurdles and convince people to share the land with grizzlies, this symbol of the American wilderness has a chance to survive.

The Endangered and Threatened Wildlife List

This series is based on the Endangered and Threatened Wildlife list compiled by the U.S. Fish and Wildlife Service (USFWS). Each book explores an endangered or threatened animal, tells why it has become endangered or threatened, and explains the efforts being made to restore the species' population.

The United States Fish and Wildlife Service, in the Department of the Interior, and the National Marine Fisheries Service, in the Department of Commerce, share responsibility for administration of the Endangered Species Act.

In 1973, Congress took the farsighted step of creating the Endangered Species Act, widely regarded as the world's strongest and most effective wildlife conservation law. It set an ambitious goal: to reverse the alarming trend of human-caused extinction that threatened the ecosystems we all share.

The complete list of Endangered and Threatened Wildlife and Plants can be found at
http://endangered.fws.gov/wildlife.html#Species.

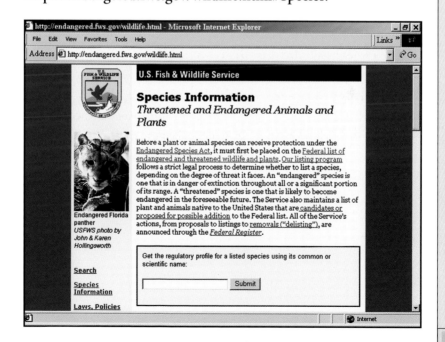

Chapter 1. The Endangered Grizzly Bear

1. *Grizzly Bear Recovery,* U.S. Fish and Wildlife Service, Mountain-Prairie Region, Lakewood, Colorado, June 2003, p. 1.

2. Ibid.

3. Ibid.

4. Ibid.

Chapter 2. "A Most Tremendious Looking Anamal"

1. Paul Schullery, *Lewis and Clark Among the Grizzlies* (Guilford, Conn.: Globe Pequot Press, 2002), p. 45.

2. Ibid., p. 46.

Chapter 3. Grizzly Bear Life

1. Douglas H. Chadwick, "Grizzlies," *National Geographic,* July 2001, p. 9.

Chapter 4. The Mythical Grizzly

1. Robert H. Busch, *The Grizzly Almanac* (New York: The Lyons Press, 2000), p. 104.

2. Ibid., p. 103.

3. Ibid., p. 104.

4. Paul Schullery, *Lewis and Clark Among the Grizzlies* (Guilford, Conn.: Globe Pequot Press, 2002), p. 62.

5. Ibid.

6. Governor Dick Kempthorne, as quoted in CNN.com, "Over Objections, Feds Plan to Release Grizzlies in Idaho Mountains," November 17, 2000, <http://archives.cnn.com/2000/NATURE/11/17/grizzly.bears.ap/> (March 3, 2005).

Further Reading

Becker, John E. *Grizzly Bears.* San Diego: Kidhaven Press, 2003.

Busch, Robert H. *Valley of the Grizzlies.* New York: St. Martin's Press, 1998.

Craighead, Lance. *Bears of the World.* Stillwater, Minn.: Voyageur Press, 2000.

Deady, Kathleen W. *Grizzly Bears.* Mankato, Minn.: Capstone Press, 2002.

Fitzgerald, Patrick J. *Bear Attacks.* New York: Children's Press, 2000.

Leach, Michael. *Grizzly Bear: Habitat, Life Cycles, Food Chains, Threats.* Austin, Tex.: Raintree Steck-Vaughn, 2001.

Lewin, Ted. *Tooth and Claw: Animal Adventures in the Wild.* New York: Harper Collins, 2003.

Miles, Victoria. *Wild Science: Amazing Encounters Between Animals and the People Who Study Them.* Vancouver, B.C.: Raincoast Books, 2004.

Patent, Dorothy Hinshaw. *Animals on the Trail With Lewis and Clark.* New York: Clarion Books, 2002.

Reading, Richard P., and Brian Miller, eds. *Endangered Animals: A Reference Guide to Conflicting Issues.* Westport, Conn.: Greenwood Press, 2000.

Russell, Charlie, and Maureen Enns. *Grizzly Seasons: Life With the Brown Bears of Kamchatka.* Buffalo: Firefly Books, 2003.

Silverstein, Alvin, Virginia Silverstein, and Laura Silverstein Nunn. *The Grizzly Bear.* Brookfield, Conn.: Millbrook Press, 1998.

Index